WHO, WHAT, WHY?

WHO WAS
MARTIN LUTHER?

CF4•K

DANIKA COOLEY

10 9 8 7 6 5 4 3 2 1
Copyright © Danika Cooley 2021
Paperback ISBN: 978-1-5271-0650-5
ebook ISBN: 978-1-5271-0823-3

Published by
Christian Focus Publications,
Geanies House, Fearn, Tain, Ross-shire,
IV20 1TW, Scotland, U.K.
www.christianfocus.com
email: info@christianfocus.com

Printed and bound by Bell and Bain, Glasgow

MIX
Paper from
responsible sources
FSC® C007785

Cover design by James Amour
Illustrations by Martyn Smith

TABLE OF CONTENTS

To Jack and Chloe.
May you always
stand for the truth
of God's Word.

THE AUTHOR

Danika Cooley and her husband, Ed, are committed to leading their children to life for the glory of God. Danika has a passion for equipping parents to teach the Bible and Christian history to their kids. She is the author of *Help Your Kids Learn and Love the Bible*, *When Lightning Struck!: The Story of Martin Luther*, *Wonderfully Made: God's Story of Life from Conception to Birth*, and the *Who, What, Why?* Series about the history of our faith. Danika's three year Bible survey curriculum, Bible Road Trip™, is used by families around the world. Weekly, she encourages tens of thousands of parents to intentionally raise biblically literate children. Danika is a homeschool mother of four with a bachelor of arts degree from the University of Washington. Find her at ThinkingKidsBlog.org.

CHANGING
THE WORLD

In the days of knights and castles, just twenty-five years after Christopher Columbus sailed the ocean blue, a thin monk from a tiny university in a smelly little town changed the world.

Why was the town smelly, you ask? Well, perhaps it was because of the stockyards just outside the city wall where farm animals were kept and butchered. With an easterly wind, the smell of blood and sweaty pigs blew across the town square and into open windows. Then again, maybe it was Wittenberg's sludgy moat that made the little city stink. That moat stood a whole city block wide and as deep as a seven-story building. In it

floated anything the citizens of Wittenberg deemed to be trash.

Our monk, whom you will come to know by the name of Martin Luther, was sent to the noxious little city surrounded by a moat on three sides and a river on the other, with a stockyard and a slaughterhouse outside the gates—and he was not impressed. Would you like to know what he sang when he thought about his "little" Wittenberg? Of course you would. He sang:

> "Little land, little land,
>
> You are but a heap of sand.
>
> If I dig you, the soil is light;
>
> If I reap you, the yield is slight."

Now, that is funny—and our monk was often a funny man—but it is not entirely true. The sandy soil of Wittenberg, Germany did grow a great many good things to eat. There were animals in the wood outside the walls that people could hunt, and of course there was the butchered meat to eat as well.

The whole town of Wittenberg would have taken you about ten minutes to stroll across. Eight city blocks wide by four city blocks long—that is all the bigger the little town was, with about four hundred clay homes covered in straw. There was a town market where citizens came to sell their vegetables, to hold medieval fairs several times a year, and even to fight when the mood took hold of them. Many people simply called the market square "The Mudhole." There were two churches as well, the city church at one side of the town and the castle church at the other. Martin referred to the worship space in which he preached as lowly, like the stall in which Jesus was born.

The University of Wittenberg where Martin taught had just over 150 students attending. It was the pet project of the local German prince, Frederick the Wise. His builder knocked down three buildings just to make room for the Friederici College building. There were classrooms on the bottom floor of the college

and about twenty dorm rooms on the top floor where the students slept. Just a few years later, the prince built the New Friederici College right next to the Old Friederici College. The new building had a small tower with a little clock, and a beer and wine tavern as well. That is where our monk Martin came to change the world.

Sometimes the people who change the world come from the most unlikely of places. Places like a little town in a little country no one paid much attention to at the time. Often the people who change the course of history are not all that important seeming until you look back and see what it is they really did with their lives.

For instance, you wouldn't guess that the son of a copper miner who was supposed to become a lawyer— but who became a poor, lowly monk instead—would create a new language, would you? Nor would you predict he would put an end to feudalism—the system of peasants, knights, and kings of the Middle Ages. You might not suppose the copper miner's son would defend the Bible and get himself in a lot of trouble with all of the important people on a whole continent.

Well, he did. Our monk did that and a whole lot more. If you go to a church now where the Bible is boldly preached, or if you have a Bible written in your own language, well, Martin had something to do with that. This is his story.

THE PRINTING PRESS

Do you enjoy copying sentences? Imagine copying an entire book by hand. In Europe during the Middle Ages, special workers called scribes painstakingly handwrote books. Naturally, books took a long time to reproduce and were very expensive.

In 1440, just forty-three years before Martin Luther was born, Johann Gutenberg—a man with an impressive mustache and beard—invented a printing press with moveable type. This meant it was easier and faster to reprint books. The first book Gutenberg printed was the Bible, the most important book in the history of the world.

The printing press was fast and not at all expensive, which helped change Europe from small, isolated towns into a connected continent. Suddenly, people could easily learn about scientific discoveries and news.

THE BIBLE

If you have a Bible, you probably already know a little about it. Many people have lost their lives defending the Bible, so let's just go over some quick facts about the world's most important book, shall we?

The Bible is the written Word of God. God's Word contains stories about God and his people, instructions for living, and the teachings of Jesus. It is always right, never wrong.

The Bible tells us God is entirely good, but people are not. Our failure to live by God's rules is called sin, and sin requires punishment. God sent his own Son, Jesus, to become fully God and fully man.

Jesus lived a life without any sin. He was crucified and buried, and three days later he rose from the dead. Believers in Jesus are forgiven for their sins because of his sacrifice, not because of anything good we do.

toddled off to school—two years earlier than most boys his age. Preschoolers are notorious for their inability to walk long distances on chubby little legs, so an older boy carried Martin on his back. At school Martin learned Latin, hymns, and Catholic prayers, along with the Bible and Aesop's Fables.

It may seem a strange mix to study stories of Jesus—who really lived—alongside tales of talking ravens and foxes, but that's the way the Middle Ages was. German peasants believed the truth of the Bible, and they also believed in elves, gnomes, and fairies. Margaretha Luther was always losing eggs, milk, and butter. You may wonder if a hungry neighbor stole from her pantry, but Martin's mother was certain evil spirits were the culprits.

Martin's parents wanted so badly for him to be a great and wealthy lawyer—and a good Catholic boy— that they whipped him over even the silliest of offenses. Once Martin took a nut from the table without asking his mother. She struck him with a stick until he bled. His father, too, whipped the boy until Martin ran away from home. Hans tracked him down and begged his forgiveness through tears. Martin forgave Hans, but never forgot his parents' anger.

At just thirteen years of age, our boy Martin walked forty miles north to the town of Magdeburg to attend a better school. At the School of the Brethren of the Common Life, Martin encountered his first real Bible. It was heavy and expensive and chained to a table so no one could take it. In the Bible, Martin read the story of Hannah. God answered Hannah's prayer for a son. She dedicated her baby, Samuel, to God, sending him to live with the priest Eli. God made young Samuel a prophet. Until then, Martin had only heard stories from the New Testament. The Old Testament was so interesting he asked God to give him a Bible of his own.

In the evenings when Martin and his classmates weren't studying, they caroled from house-to-house. In the Middle Ages wealthy boys commonly sang for

their supper. Today we have television, books, and even board games to keep us busy at home, but this was not the case for medieval families. They loved the entertainment carolers provided so much they handed out food as a reward. Caroling allowed Martin to earn his dinner while he was attending school.

While Martin was singing for his supper, he met a monk who changed the way he saw life altogether. The man was all skin and bone, holding a sack so heavy he could not stand up straight even once he set it down—he was permanently bent. This sad monk was none other than Prince William of Anhalt. The prince believed, as most Roman Catholics did, becoming a monk or a nun was the best way to serve God and gain entrance to heaven. He spent his days begging for food for his fellow monks. Martin felt shame over his own life. Was he really pleasing God in becoming a lawyer? He didn't think he was.

Martin's parents still wanted him to become a wealthy attorney, so off he went to an even better school in the city of Eisenach. At the Latin School of Saint George's Church, one of Martin's all-time favorite teachers, Headmaster Trebonius, would remove his hat as his students entered the room. He would say, "You boys are the future mayors, officials, rulers, and doctors of Germany!" That would be a fun thing to hear about yourself, wouldn't it?

Headmaster Trebonius likely had no idea one of his very own students would change the history of the entire world.

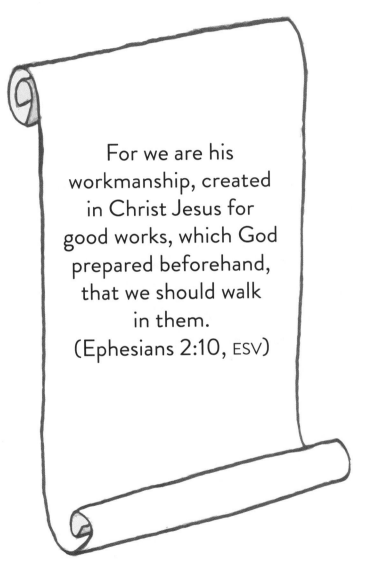

For we are his workmanship, created in Christ Jesus for good works, which God prepared beforehand, that we should walk in them.
(Ephesians 2:10, ESV)

THE MEDIEVAL ROMAN CATHOLIC CHURCH

The medieval Roman Catholic Church taught that the pope—the head of the Church—could not be wrong when he spoke about faith or morals. Cardinals helped the pope and oversaw archbishops, who supervised bishops, who were the leaders of priests. Monks and nuns were humble Church servants.

The Church struggled with corruption. Church offices were sold for money and favors. Some leaders—including popes—did not keep their promise to remain single or poor. Also, priests told people they could purchase a paper and their sins would be forgiven. Some scholars and Church officials cried out for reform, but they were ignored.

POPE

CARDINAL

ARCH BISHOP

BISHOP

PRIEST

MONK   NUN

A PHILOSOPHER

In the spring of 1501, seventeen-year-old Martin walked fifty miles south of his home in Mansfeld to attend the University of Erfurt. It was half a year before Michelangelo began carving the seventeen-foot-tall marble statue of King David. Erfurt sat in a valley surrounded by fields of blue, purple, and yellow plants used to dye fabric. Martin probably first saw a giant cathedral on a hill in the very middle of the city.

There were Roman Catholic churches, monasteries, convents, and chapels, too—more than one hundred, in fact. He would have noticed the uneven crushed-stone streets with houses jutting into the road and random dead ends forcing travelers to try again to reach their destinations. Amongst the church buildings, tile-roofed shops, and random clay homes wound canals covered by footbridges. The few little university buildings sat on a small stream.

Martin learned about literature, physics, and theology—the study of God. The university taught

about God using the Bible, works of early Christians, and writings of non-Christian thinkers. This bothered Martin—later in his life he argued only the Bible should be used to study God. That idea plunged Martin into some hot water, but we're not quite to that part of the story yet.

Martin was always looking for ways to have fun. But Martin really, truly loved to win. Debating was an important skill at the university. Martin was quick with his words. He argued so well during debates his friends called him "The Philosopher."

Remember the story of Prince William of Anhalt? He walked away from his kingdom to become a monk. Martin remembered him too. When Martin wasn't joking around or winning a debate, he was worrying about heaven and hell. Was Martin doing enough to please God?

Martin excelled at school, earning a bachelor's degree in philosophy at the end of 1502. When he began studies for his master's degree, things started to go awry.

April 16, 1503 was just a few weeks before Christopher Columbus happened upon the sea-turtle-laden Cayman Islands during his fourth voyage across the Atlantic Ocean. Martin and a friend began walking home to see Hans and Margaretha. Martin carried a sword for protection. In the Middle Ages, a sword was a necessity—there were robbers on the roads.

It's possible Martin wasn't paying attention, or the ground was still icy from winter. We may never know what made Martin trip and fall on the hillside above Erfurt. When he fell, his sword stabbed him deeply in the leg. Martin pulled the sword from his badly swollen leg. He did the best thing he could have with a severed cephalic vein—he put his thumb inside the wound and pressed on the vein while his friend ran back to Erfurt. Instead of praying to Jesus, Martin called out to Saint Mary.

A group of Martin's friends carried him back to the university. A doctor from a nearby village operated, yet Martin nearly died. In fact, his leg burst open and had to be sewn closed again. The pain must have been unimaginable.

Do you remember I said things went awry for Martin? Well, getting stabbed in the leg was just the

beginning. Martin survived his brush with death, but his friends were not as fortunate. The Black Death came to Erfurt and countless people died, including fellow students. At the same time, typhoid fever infected many citizens. Martin's dear friend Hieronymus Buntz died from a swelling around his lungs.

It's one thing to wonder if there might be a monster in the closet—it's another thing entirely to watch your friends die. Terrified, Martin thought more and more often about heaven, hell, and salvation. Our philosopher grew resentful with God, seeing him as an angry judge rather than as a loving Father.

Two years after his sword injury—in June of 1505, in case you love dates—Martin visited Hans and Margaretha for ten days, celebrating. Martin had just earned a Master's degree, he would be a lawyer, and he was engaged to be married. It seemed Martin's life was just about to get good.

On his walk back to the University of Erfurt to attend Law School, it began to rain—a furious, howling rain. A massive clap of thunder sounded and lightning filled the sky. Martin knew it was very dangerous to be caught outside in a thunderstorm, and he was still a long way from the university.

Our law student ran down the road and took shelter beneath an elm tree. The thick canopy of leaves must have seemed to him to be a good place to hide from the storm. Martin probably did not know lightning will always travel down a conduit—a path to the ground. Trees make good conduits as they are very tall. So there Martin was,

huddling beneath the elm tree, when a bolt of lightning found its conduit. The elm burst into flames and split in half. Martin was thrown violently to the ground and momentarily blinded.

Afraid for his life, Martin called out to Anna, the patron saint of miners. "Help, Saint Anna! Save me. I will become a monk."

THE BLACK DEATH

During the mid-1300s, plague-infected rats traveled to Europe from Mongolia on ships and in military wagons. The fleas on the sick rats bit people, spreading the illness to humans.

The Black Death wasn't like a regular cold. Infected people would get black boils all over their skin. These blisters would swell with blood and pus until they burst. That's when victims became truly ill before dying. The Death spread quickly. Doctors wore strange hoods for protection while treating patients—if they didn't just leave town when the plague arrived.

Historians argue over how many people died each time the Black Death spread, but they agree it was devastating. Imagine a family of five losing two or three people. The Black Death was a cruel enemy.

O, HOLY ROME

If I told you the whole of Martin Luther's story, this would be a very long book. After all, most people do many things in their lives, and the years go by one day at a time. We last left our young man Martin in a thunderstorm, beneath an elm tree hit by lightning.

He promised Saint Anna, a dead woman, he would become a monk. Our Martin was many things—competitive, proud, often angry—but he was not a liar. Just two weeks after his lost fight with the thunderstorm, Martin threw himself a goodbye party with his best guy friends in attendance. He did, after all, love to celebrate. Our almost-lawyer sold his

lawbooks, gave away his lute, and entered the strictest monastery he could find.

Now, being a monk was not easy. Martin promised to eat very little, pray late into the night, remain poor while wearing a scratchy hair cloak, and beg for his food. Even so, Martin managed to make his difficult job harder. You see, our monk Martin thought by living a very difficult life, he could earn the favor and grace of God. That is just silly. The Bible says the grace of God is a gift we do not deserve and cannot earn, but Martin did not know this. He laid on the freezing stone floor, often eating nothing at all. He resolved not to sleep, once staying awake for five weeks without even a nap. How Martin survived, we may never know.

An argument broke out between the Augustinian monks, so Martin was sent to Rome to help end the fight. Now, Rome is in Italy, and Martin's monastery was in Erfurt, Germany. Between the two cities lay the Alps, a stretch of mountains curving from France through Slovenia. Martin walked over these mountains in the dead of winter, more than 850 miles in the deep snow, in order to reach the capital of the Roman Catholic world.

You would think Martin would be tired, cold, and afraid. But Martin was excited. He really wanted to go to heaven. After all, he'd become a monk to please God. In Rome were all kinds of things a monk could do to earn the favor of God and spend less time in purgatory—kind of like a checklist of good deeds. The Roman Catholic Church taught purgatory was a place where people went to be punished for their sins, sometimes for millions of years, before being released to heaven. It's not a real place, but Martin believed it was, and he did not want to go there.

In one day, Martin visited the seven most important churches in Rome. He saw the catacombs—tunnels where the bones of Christians were buried. Martin viewed the skulls of the saints and even drank water from a spring that flowed over saintly bones. He told, or confessed, his sins to a priest who just yawned.

But wait—there's more. Martin saw the Samaritan woman's grave, a chain from the apostle Paul's imprisonment, a rope tied to Jesus when he was crucified, and eleven thorns from the crown that pierced Jesus' head. Our monk saw the sponge used to give Jesus a drink on the cross, and a nail from the crucifixion. He viewed a piece of the burning bush and Moses' staff. All of this and much more, Martin saw in Rome.

Rather than building Martin's faith and bringing him peace, all the relics—that is what the Roman

35

Catholic Church called their many old things— all those pieces of bone, rope, and cloth made Martin uneasy. Perhaps his holy checklist was not quite so real. Maybe God didn't care if Martin prayed in front of pieces of bone.

Martin ended his trip to Rome climbing the stairs that led to Pontius Pilate's house. Remember Pilate from the Bible? He is right there in every gospel. Matthew 27, Mark 15, Luke 23, and John 18-19 tell the story of the Roman governor who crucified Jesus even though Jesus was innocent. Well, Pilate's headquarters were in Jerusalem, Israel, yet here was Martin—climbing Pilate's stairs in the middle of Rome, Italy.

Martin climbed the stairs on his knees, saying the Lord's Prayer on every step. Each prayer on each step was supposed to let someone out of purgatory nine years early. There were twenty-eight steps, so Martin prayed that someone could be released from purgatory 252 years early.

When Martin got to the top of the stairs, his knees hurt and he was confused about why a good and loving

God would make his people do something so strange in order to earn God's favor. Martin stood at the top of the steps and questioned, "Who knows whether this is true?"

That, my friend, is when our monk Martin's life started to get interesting. Martin was about to meet Jesus. Not a rope that might have touched Jesus—but Jesus, the Son of God and God-made-man. The real Jesus.

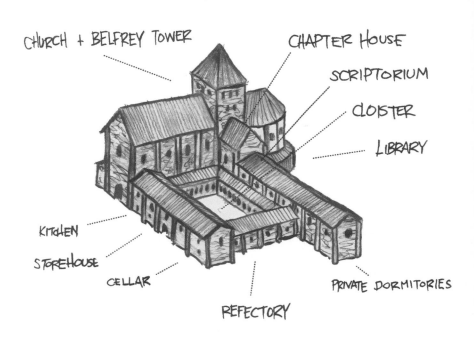

CHURCH + BELFREY TOWER

CHAPTER HOUSE

SCRIPTORIUM

CLOISTER

LIBRARY

KITCHEN

STOREHOUSE

CELLAR

PRIVATE DORMITORIES

REFECTORY

MEDIEVAL MONASTERIES

About a hundred years after Jesus ascended to heaven, a few people decided things like food, sleep, and soft clothes might keep them from worshiping properly. Soon others wanted to live simple lives, too, so men started monasteries and women started convents—small villages where monks or nuns lived, worked, and worshiped together. Monks gave food to the poor, copied books by hand, cared for the elderly, sick, and orphaned, and paid for artwork to be created.

With lots of men or women living and worshiping together and trying to be holy, there needed to be some rules—pages and pages of rules. Monks couldn't agree on the rules, so there were different kinds of monasteries, each with their own set of rules.

THE NINETY-
FIVE THESES

The problem with Martin, his friends may have told you, was he didn't know when to let something go. He wanted to teach truth, but the medieval Church cared more about tradition than the truth in the Bible. But Martin loved a good debate, and one was about to find him.

On the way from Rome, Italy to Germany's Erfurt and then Wittenberg, our monk stayed at monasteries along the way. He saw many of the same relics he prayed over in Rome. He began to wonder how many crowns of thorns Jesus really wore to the cross. It seemed there were many in existence.

The summer of 1510, Martin was sent to teach the Bible to students at the University of Wittenberg, the tiny university in the stinky little town where Martin changed the world. He spent a good deal of time reading the red leather Bible given to him by Dr. Staupitz. It was in that Bible that Martin found the truth.

Martin was beginning to suspect he could not be saved from his sins by sleeping on a cold floor, praying on his face, or confessing his sins hourly. Our Martin was teaching the book of Romans to students a little older than you when he came across Romans 1:17, which says, "... as it is written, the just shall live by faith."

That's when Martin finally knew—Jesus did not want Martin's good deeds as admission to heaven. All of Martin's righteousness was just filthy rags to Jesus. Martin finally believed in Jesus as the Son of God and God-made-man for his salvation. He understood God so loved the world he sent his one and only Son Jesus to die in our place. Martin believed and confessed his belief with his mouth. He was saved and repented of his sins.

Now, a saved man cannot keep the wonder and glory of God to himself, and Martin just happened to have a pulpit from which to preach. His students heard two earfuls daily about the grace and glory of God. Professors, priests, and even princes came to hear Martin speak about the truth of Jesus, our Savior.

In 1516, Martin preached three times against the Church practice of selling indulgences while the Black Plague swept through Wittenberg. An indulgence was a piece of paper that is supposed to give the purchaser a little help toward salvation. Martin preached from the Bible about God's grace—God's free gift of salvation to all who believe in Jesus.

That same year, Pope Leo X in Rome ran out of money. The pope had raised money for a crusade—a war he called holy—by selling indulgences. Alas, he spent the money for his war on other things like

gambling and pies filled with live nightingales that flew out of the center when the crust was cut. Leo needed more money. He was paying Michelangelo to paint the ceiling of the Sistine Chapel, Raphael to paint murals of Roman legends with Leo's face on all the important characters, and he wanted to finish the building of St. Peter's Basilica—the largest church building in the world.

Leo X may not have been able to save a penny, but he was very good at fundraising. So, he sold offices in the Church to men who wanted to be bishops and cardinals, he sold knighthood to men who wanted a coat of arms, and he sold indulgences to any common person who wanted to be forgiven their sins.

Leo sent a dumpy little monk named Tetzel to a town just one day's walk northeast of Martin's Wittenberg. Tetzel swept into town preaching about the horrors of being tortured in purgatory, then announced one's sins could be forgiven through the purchase of a special indulgence from the pope.

When Martin heard of Tetzel's indulgence sale, he was livid. He made a list of points, called theses, of things wrong with the pope's sale of indulgences. It was silly for the money of German peasants to build a decorated church in Italy. The pope does not have the power to forgive sins. Saints have no extra credits or merit. We are forgiven by Jesus, saved by grace through the faith God gives us. Lastly, our debater Martin pointed out people who thought they were forgiven because they paid money for salvation might never really believe in Jesus and be saved.

On October 31st—All Saint's Eve—in 1517, Martin nailed the Ninety-Five Theses to the door of the Wittenberg Castle Church where it was sure to be seen by scholars and students. The list was also seen by a local printer. He translated it from scholarly Latin into German, printed many copies, and sent it to be nailed to church doors and platforms in market squares across Germany, Italy, France—all of Europe.

That is how our fiery little monk Martin, who lived in a smelly little town and preached at a tiny little university, picked a fight with the most powerful man in all the world.

PURGATORY AND INDULGENCES

The Church taught people were saved by credit earned through good deeds. Most Christians couldn't do enough good works, so they would be purified through punishment in purgatory before heaven, rather than by the blood of Jesus.

The Church taught Jesus had an abundance of merit. The Church gave Jesus' credit to believers, then began selling credit in the form of an indulgence. Pope Leo X signed plenary indulgences, which were supposed to grant the buyer full forgiveness of their sins.

Are purgatory and indulgences in the Bible? No. God's Word says we are saved by God's grace through faith in Jesus Christ.

Romans 10:9-11 says, "… if you confess with your mouth that Jesus is Lord and believe in your heart that God raised him from the dead, you will be saved. For with the heart one believes and is justified, and with the mouth one confesses and is saved. For the Scripture says, "Everyone who believes in him will not be put to shame."

A DIET OF
WORMS?

Powerful men don't like to be challenged by backwater monks. Pope Leo X was no different. Martin's Theses were translated into new languages and people from all over Europe read them. At first, Leo was annoyed. He received letters from powerful rulers, telling him to stop

his disrespectful monk from speaking. Leo made a new rule. To speak against the pope was to break the law.

Leo did not know Martin well. Martin published tracts, sermons—even a book—defending his Theses. He continued teaching Jesus is the only way to salvation. Frustrated, Leo sent Martin to apologize to a cardinal in Augsburg. Martin barely escaped with his life, fleeing through a hole in the wall in the dead

of night. Next, Leo let Martin debate a theologian for eighteen days. Supporters for both sides were outraged when no one was declared the winner.

In 1520, Martin wrote books about the way the Roman Catholic Church was misusing money and over-taxing common people. He criticized the rules of the Church, explained the freedom we have in Christ, and reminded people we are saved by God's grace.

Leo threw Martin out of the Roman Catholic Church. For a Catholic that meant going to hell. But Martin no longer believed the pope could send him to hell.

Germany was part of twenty-one-year-old Charles V's empire. Some German princes were loyal to the pope, while others were willing to risk their kingdoms for the gospel. While German princes were arguing over salvation, Turkish armies were making their way up the Danube River. Emperor Charles V needed the German

princes to fight the Turks, or he might lose the Eastern side of his territory.

The emperor called a meeting of rulers in the empire. The council met in the city of Worms. The Diet of Worms is a funny name, but it had nothing to do with eating anything from the phylum annelida—those ringed, squishy creatures that live in the soil of your garden.

Had Martin not been supported by so many German princes, knights, and common people, Charles could have put Martin to death and moved on with attacking the Turks. As it was, Germany—maybe all of Europe—was close to civil war.

The city of Worms in mid-February of 1521 was in disarray. German townspeople chanted "Luther!" in the streets while the rest yelled, "Die, Romans!" A man with eighty-five books written by Martin peddled his wares in the road. He was beaten by Spanish knights, his books destroyed. The next day, those knights were attacked by German townspeople.

Three months into the Diet of Worms, Charles V convinced Martin to speak for himself before the council. The day Martin arrived—after two weeks of preaching on the way—the people of Germany had filled the city to overflowing. Each bed held six or seven people. Even the Emperor shared a room with his advisor. That night, princes from throughout Germany came to visit Martin, expressing their support for the gospel.

The next morning, Martin was hurried to a room to stand trial before Charles V, German princes, the Spanish court, and officials from the Roman Catholic Church. The hearing was packed. Outside, people waited anxiously in the street.

"Have you written these books? Will you apologize for them?" The lawyer motioned to a pile.

Martin's lawyer insisted all the titles be read aloud. Martin listened to twenty-five titles read. "Those are mine. I've written more."

Our fiery monk-turned-preacher knew if he did not apologize for opposing the Church, he would be deemed a heretic. He could be burned at the stake, which is a terrible way to die. If he apologized for his work, on the other hand, would he not be denying the work of Jesus on the cross? Martin asked for more time to pray.

These mighty men of Europe had been debating for three months now—our man Martin wanted another day to decide? Shouldn't he know his answer by now? Martin was sent to his room until the following evening. The next day, Martin explained. "I have three kinds of books. The first kind teaches people how to live as Christians. No one disagrees with these.

"The second kind talks about the unbiblical teachings of the Church. I cannot apologize for these."

Emperor Charles stood and yelled, "No!"

Holy Roman Emperors and Roman Catholic popes were close allies in running Europe, and the emperor— of course—wanted Martin to deny his teachings.

Martin frowned. "The third type of book attacks people. Those people attacked the truth, and I cannot apologize!" Now, Martin was cranky with anyone who disagreed with him, and his insults were even crankier. He said things your mom would not want you to repeat in public or in private, but he was—in his opinion— defending the truth.

"You consider yourself smarter than the Church?" The Roman lawyer was cranky, too. "Apologize for your lies!"

That is when Martin said his most famous words. "I must be convinced by the Bible or logic, not by popes or councils. My conscience belongs to the Word of God! I will not apologize. I cannot go against my conscience."

KING

NOBLE

KNIGHT

PEASANT

FEUDALISM

Government is how nations decide who's in charge and what the rules are. There are many kinds of government, like socialism, democratic republics, and monarchies. Feudalism was the form of government used in the Roman Empire from the 800s to the 1400s AD.

In the Middle Ages, most people never traveled outside their town. The economy and government in Europe was based on local farming. Rich nobles, called lords, owned plots of land called fiefs. Peasants, or vassals, grew food on a portion of a noble's land. In return, they owed much of the food they grew to the lord of the fief. The lords hired warriors, called knights, to protect their fiefs and vassals. Most of the time peasants owned nothing and didn't have enough to eat.

KIDNAPPED!

Martin wasn't burned at the stake in Worms. He was, however, declared a heretic and an outlaw. The emperor gave him three weeks of safe travel to Wittenberg before anyone could begin the stake burning. At least he would die at home, Martin thought.

Martin and his friends stopped at German towns to preach on the way home. In the forest of Thuringia,

near his uncle Heinz's house, Martin preached to poor townspeople before spending the night with his family. In the morning, his wagon traveled along the Gotha Highway, past Schweina Road and the Castle Altenstein.

Martin spotted a group of horsemen with drawn swords galloping from behind the castle's little chapel building. I don't know if you've ever been in a wagon in the woods surrounded by armed horsemen with a bounty on your head, but I imagine it is terrifying. One of Martin's friends certainly felt this way. He leapt from the wagon and fled into the dark woods. The wagon's driver stood and pointed at Martin. For his trouble, he was hit upside the head with the hard end of a crossbow, which knocked him under the wagon.

As Martin was thrown across a horse, he grabbed his Hebrew Old Testament and his Greek New Testament. The armed horsemen stowed Martin in the locked tower room of the Wartburg Castle, high above Eisenach.

The sound of bats and an owl winging through his room kept Martin company.

Now, you might be wondering about the identities of these terrible men who kidnapped our preacher. Prince Frederick the Wise of Saxony, overseer of the University of Wittenberg where Martin taught, was more than a little concerned his prize lecturer was now a wanted outlaw—able to be executed by any man on the street. Frederick was a practical man. Martin brought new students, fame, and royal attention to the little town of Wittenberg in the province of Saxony. This was good for business. Martin's preaching—well, that had been good for Prince Frederick's soul. When

it looked as though the man preaching the gospel may be killed, Frederick had him thrown in a tower.

Our Martin never backed down from a fight. Indeed, when he said, "My conscience belongs to the Word of God!" he really and truly meant he was ready and willing to die for the gospel. Our former monk was spitting mad when the sun rose on his little tower room—which he called his Patmos, the kingdom of the birds, in the realm of the air.

With nothing else to do, Martin read his Hebrew Old Testament and Greek New Testament daily. Three weeks later, he shipped off a commentary on Psalm 68 to be published. Until then, it's fair to say the people of Germany, Rome—all of Europe—likely thought Martin was dead, killed for his views. Now they knew he was alive, but they did not know where he could be hiding.

Martin wrote about the Magnificat, where Mary praises our great God. Mary was not a sinless saint as the Roman Catholic Church taught. She was merely a regular saint like you or I, chosen by God, trusting in his grace. Next, Martin taught about the priesthood of believers—we are all brothers and sisters in Christ. While in prison Martin wrote about marriage, preaching, and how pastors should live. His books were smuggled into Wittenberg, published, and sent throughout all of Europe.

Martin translated the New Testament from Greek into German in just under three months. Now, maybe that doesn't sound like a big deal, but if your mom ever made you learn Greek, you know the alphabet looks like pictures. It's quite difficult to learn. Also, there were several variations of the German language. There was royal court German, peasant German, and German for small towns no one ever visited. So, Martin made his own German—and everyone in Germany decided to use it. Translating the Bible is one thing. Inventing a language is another. Martin did both.

Outside the walls of Martin's Patmos, things were getting radical as Martin wrote about Christian freedom. Nuns and monks were marrying each other. Common people were taking communion with both the wine and the bread. These things were against Roman Catholic rules. In Wittenberg, Catholic Mass—the service performed by priests— was outlawed. Monks grew out their hair, quit praying for the dead, stopped visiting relics, worshiped God in services spoken in German rather than Latin, ate meat on fasting days, and smashed saintly statues they used to pray to.

Peasants and students also became involved. With swords, they slashed books of Mass, chased priests from the chapel of the church, and threw rocks at worshipers praying to Mary. Piling high pictures of saints and angels, the mob set fire to the pile, then threw the altars on top for good measure.

This was the last straw for Martin. Sneaking away from prison, Martin returned home and preached eight days straight.

"You have faith. But without love, faith is false!"

Dieu est amour

Gott ist
Liebe

бог есть
любовь

God is
Love

BIBLE TRANSLATIONS

The language you grow up speaking is your "heart language." We have over 450 English Bible translations, but there was a long period when people could only read the Bible in Latin. Scholars could study the original Hebrew and Greek manuscripts—if they could find them.

The Bible is inspired (written by God through men), inerrant (never wrong), and infallible (it can never be wrong). The Bible tells us God is King—powerful over every person, nation, and event. He created people for his glory. People sinned and were separated from God, but God had a plan for salvation through Jesus. We read in the Bible about Jesus' commands to us.

Because of the Reformers, you can read the Bible in your heart language and understand what it says.

Is gràdh Dia

A WAR, A WIFE,
AND A FUNERAL

During this free-for-all, a German nun named Katie found freedom in Christ. Katharina von Bora lived in the Cistercian Cloister in Saxony. All forty nuns were forbidden to speak, and leaving the convent came with the promise of execution. Friendships were not allowed.

Perhaps you wonder how Katie came to be in this situation. The girl was only five when her mother died, and ten when her father remarried. Like many poor or unwanted girls, Katie was sent to spend her life in silence.

Katie read the writings of Martin Luther and put her faith in Jesus. She wrote to Martin asking him to rescue her. Our pastor recruited the help of a most unlikely ally, Leonard Koppe—a traveling merchant who delivered food to Katie's convent.

The night before Easter in 1523, Koppe stuffed Katie, her aunt who ran the convent, and ten of their fellow nuns into empty herring and beer barrels. The ladies must have smelled dreadful by the end of their journey in the back of the merchant's wagon. Three

of the nuns were dropped off with their fathers. Katie and the remaining ladies landed on Martin's doorstep.

Katie wasn't the shy, retiring type of girl you might envision a medieval peasant nun to be. She was energetic and determined. Katie wanted to be a part of God's work in the Reformation, and she wanted a wise, godly husband. She told Martin she would marry either him or his friend, Dr. Amsdorf. Martin thought he'd make "the angels laugh and the devil weep" if he followed God's plan for marriage. He'd been telling others to marry and have children—why shouldn't he?

While Martin was rescuing Katie, the gospel was spreading. Many people heard they could profess Jesus, turn from their sins, and be saved. Still, not everyone heard the same message. Many German peasants heard a message of social upheaval.

As pastors spoke against the abuses of the Roman Catholic Church, peasants began to think about the abuses of the nobility. They wanted to be free to hunt and fish on the land they rented. They wanted fair rent, fair wages, and commands that came only from God's Word. Instead, peasants worked hard and starved harder. It was a bitter, brutal life in which they lost much.

During this time, a certain Countess of Lütphen decided she simply must have strawberries for a banquet. She ordered her serfs to pick the fruit on a holy day when they should have been celebrating. This did not go over well with her peasants. They marched on nearby towns armed with tools, and recruited more starving, angry peasants to join them.

Martin got involved, telling noblemen to treat the peasants fairly, and telling the peasants to obey their nobles. Later, as the peasants attacked monasteries, Martin called them "bands of hell," and "murderous, thieving hordes." By the end of the German Peasant War, 270 castles and 122 monasteries were ransacked. Wealthy families were slain. Knights and nobles retaliated, killing as many peasants as they could find. Some say more than 100,000 people died.

Did Martin add to the anger? Some people think he did. During the war, Martin and Katie married with a parade through town, a dinner in the Black Cloister, and a dance in the town hall.

When their son, Hans, was just over a year old, pregnant Katie survived a bout of the Black Plague. Martin wrote the hymn "A Mighty Fortress is Our God" during this time, as the family struggled to survive their illness. Little Elizabeth was born but did not live long.

Still, Martin and Katie lived a happy, busy life in their former monastery. While Martin wrote, preached, and helped with the Reformation, Katie took care of their overflowing household. She worked hard on the garden Martin bought her, growing fruit trees and vegetables of all kinds. She stocked the pond with different kinds of fish and kept hens, ducks, pigs, and cows.

Why so much gardening and farming? The Luther home had five living children, plus four orphaned

adoptees, with foster children who came and went. There were tutors for the kids, Martin's sister's family and his great niece, Katie's Aunt Lena, nuns and monks who'd left their convents and monasteries, widows, university students, and visitors hoping to learn from Martin. Every dinner at Martin and Katie's home fed at least twenty to thirty people.

Sometimes Martin would bowl with his family and guests out on the lawn or play a game of chess. There was a lot of singing and music in the Black Cloister. Still, Martin was ill from many years of starving himself, and tired from leading a reformation of the Church as an outlaw from a little town in Germany. He was frequently cranky and often angry. He wrote things he shouldn't have, and angered people who ought to have been his friends.

It was 1542 when the Luthers' beloved teen daughter Magdalena became terribly ill. Her head was hot and sweaty, and she struggled to stay awake. Martin prayed to God, "I love her so much, but if taking Lena is your will, I give her to you." When Magdalena died, Katie cried for days, and Martin was never the same.

TABLE TALKS

Martin loved to talk, and he said much in many colorful ways. His students thought Martin's sayings should be recorded. They scribbled down Martin's "table talk" at dinner and breakfast, or in their rooms each evening.

Later, Martin's stories were edited into a book. It's one of the ways we know so much about his life. Look at some of Martin's sayings:

"The Bible is alive, it speaks to me; it has feet, it runs after me; it has hands, it lays hold of me."

"The god of the world is riches, pleasure, and pride, wherewith it abuses all the creatures and gifts of God."

"Faith is the 'yes' of the heart, a conviction on which one stakes one's life."

"If I rest, I rust."

THE REFORMATION
SPREADS

When you read a story in a book, you'll find it has a beginning, a middle, and an end. The plot will be neatly tied up in a bow, and the main character will travel a satisfying character arc. He'll want something very badly and he'll work hard to get the thing he wants. While pursuing his deepest desire, the character will become a better person.

Real life is messier. In the grand story of the Church, there are people whom God uses to his glory. God grows their character. He preserves his people, his Word to us, and his great plan for salvation. But there are always many things happening at the same time, with lots of characters working for the Lord. It's fun to learn more about the people of God's story and how they interact. We learn more about how God works in our lives and in our world.

As Martin Luther was studying the Bible, praying for hours a day, and writing, others were reading. How long is your favorite book? One hundred pages? Let's say that's right. Martin Luther wrote more than 600 times as many books in his lifetime—over 60,000 pages. Yet, he was never paid for any of his books. Instead, printers took Martin's words, translated them into common languages, and distributed his work across Europe.

Scholars, farmers, and housewives read what Martin had to say about the fact that salvation is a gift from God that comes through the faith God gives us. They learned the Bible is the only source of wisdom we really need. Kings and the pope read Martin's teachings that we can talk directly to Jesus in prayer. We don't need

to confess our sins to a priest or pay the pope for our salvation. Jesus deals directly with us and the Holy Spirit is our Helper.

Good news has a way of getting out, and this was very good news indeed. By 1519, just two years after Martin nailed the Ninety-Five Theses to the door of the Castle Church, a priest named Ulrich Zwingli began the movement for reform in Switzerland. In 1522, the year Martin escaped his prison in the Wartburg Castle, Zwingli began preaching sermons based on the New Testament. Zwingli would later die fighting in the Battle of Kappel for the right to follow the Bible.

In 1521 a charismatic sect of early Anabaptists, the Zwickau Prophets, stormed into Wittenberg. Rather than relying on human tradition and councils like the Roman Catholic Church, or on Scripture like the Protestant Reformers, these men trusted dreams and visions. They were radical in their ideas and in the way they carried them out—often using violence.

In 1523, the Reformation movement's first two martyrs were burned at the stake in Belgium for daring to preach the truth. By 1526, the next year, Reformation sparked in Denmark. Norway officially became Lutheran, though it took the people of Norway until 1604 to accept reform. The next year,

John Calvin had written his first copy of Institutes, volumes on how to live biblically. The Reformation reached Sweden by 1527 and continued to spread across Switzerland through the late 1520s.

The Reformation traveled even to Iceland, an island in the cold waters of the North Sea, by 1533. The Icelandic Reformation was established in the late 1530s. In 1536, William Tyndale—who translated the Bible into English, probably some of it while staying with Martin and Katie—was burned at the stake by

King Henry VIII. His translation was later used as the basis of the King James Bible. By the late 1540s, Reformers such as John Knox in Scotland were suffering persecution and martyrdom.

Calvinist missionaries carried the Calvinistic Reformation throughout Europe in the 1550s, arriving in France, Scotland, Poland, England, Transylvania— now Romania, and the Netherlands. They worked throughout the 1560s, spreading God's Word to Hungary.

The journey of the Reformation of the Church was rocky and often violent. But the good news of Jesus Christ went forth, spreading and taking root everywhere it landed. Across Europe, common people were able to hear and read the Bible in their own language. They understood God saves his people by his grace through the faith he gives, they worshiped Jesus, and prayed to God alone.

Martin continued his work to reform the Church until the day of his death on the 18th of February in 1546. Never one to stay out of the public eye, he was involved in solving a political dispute when he died.

God's truth never stays hidden for long. It's a truth worth staking our lives upon, worth fighting for, and worth studying daily. Martin and Katie Luther loved Jesus. Because of their faithful witness, today we can stand on this truth: We are saved by grace through faith.

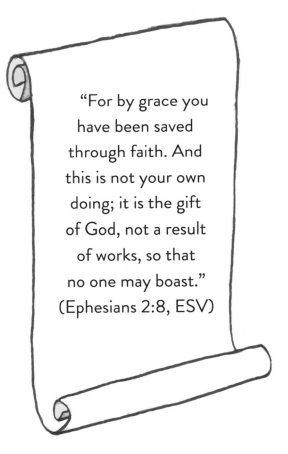

"For by grace you have been saved through faith. And this is not your own doing; it is the gift of God, not a result of works, so that no one may boast." (Ephesians 2:8, ESV)

THE PROTESTANT CHURCH

In 1529, Emperor Charles V declared the entire Holy Roman Empire must be Catholic. Martin and his colleagues wrote a statement of faith, and the German princes presented the statement to Charles V, protesting his ruling. They were called Protestants because of their protest.

All Protestants agree upon three things. First, the Bible is the authoritative Word of God. We can trust every word the Bible says, and we should not add to it. Second, we are saved by Jesus Christ alone by grace through faith—not by works. Third, every Christian is a priest and a saint. We all read the Bible, take care of other Christians, and share the gospel.

Though different Protestant denominations differ in belief on minor doctrine, all Protestant Christians believe these three things because we read them in Scripture.

TIMELINE

1483

Martin Luther is born in Eisleben, Germany. He is baptized into the Roman Catholic Church.

1484

Hans and Margaretha move Martin to Mansfeld, Germany.

Diego Cam from Portugal sails to the mouth of the Congo River.

1492

The Spanish Inquisition gives Jews three months to convert to Christianity or flee the country.

Leonardo da Vinci illustrates a flying machine.

Christopher Columbus sails from Spain and finds the Bahamas, Cuba, and Hispaniola.

Martin goes to school in Mansfeld.

1495

Da Vinci begins painting "The Last Supper" in Italy.

Jews are kicked out of Portugal.

1497

Vasco de Gama sails around the Cape of Good Hope, arriving in India in 1498.

Martin attends school in Magdeburg.

1498

Martin goes to school in Eisenach.

1499

Political cartoons appear for the first time.

1500

Pig Surgeon Jakob Nufer delivers the first known baby by Caesarean section.

1501

The Pope orders all books that do not support Church teaching to be burned.

Printing presses spread, producing over 10 million copies of more than 35,000 books since 1445.

Amerigo Vespucci realizes South America and India are different continents.

Martin begins studies at the University of Erfurt.

1502

Martin graduates from the University of Erfurt with a bachelor's degree.

1505

Martin earns a master's degree from Erfurt.

Martin is trapped in a thunderstorm and vows to become a monk.

Martin enters the Augustinian Monastery at Erfurt.

1507

Martin Luther is ordained as a Roman Catholic priest.

1509

Henry VIII becomes King of England.

Roman Empire authorizes burning Jewish religious books. Jews are persecuted in Germany.

Roman Catholic Bishop Las Casas begins the slave trade, directing Spanish settlers to bring slaves from Africa to the New World.

1510

Martin sees the depravity of the Roman Catholic Church in Rome.

1511

Martin teaches at Wittenberg University.

1512

Martin earns his Doctor of Divinity.

Copernicus writes the earth and planets go around the sun, rather than the sun and planets revolving around the earth.

Michelangelo finishes painting the ceiling of the Sistine Chapel in Rome.

1513

Giovanni de' Medici becomes Pope Leo X in Rome.

Vasco Núñez de Balboa finds the Panama Isthmus and the Pacific Ocean.

Martin begins lecturing on the Psalms.

1515

Martin begins teaching Romans. He is the district vicar for 10 monasteries.

1516

Martin teaches Galatians.

1517

Johann Tetzel sells indulgences by order of Pope Leo X.

Martin posts The Ninety-Five Theses on the Wittenberg Castle Church door.

Martin teaches Hebrews.

1518

Martin meets with Cardinal Cajetan at the Diet of Augsburg.

Raphael paints a portrait of Pope Leo X with his cardinals.

Lorens de Gominot is licensed to bring 4,000 African slaves to Spanish colonies in the Americas.

1519

Martin debates Johann Eck at the Leipzig Disputation.

Hernando Cortés of Spain meets with Aztec Emperor Montezuma in Tenochtitlán, Mexico.

Ulrich Zwingli begins preaching on the New Testament in Switzerland.

1520

Pope Leo X excommunicates Martin.

Lucas Cranach paints Martin's portrait.

Charles V becomes the Holy Roman Emperor at age 19.

Thomas Münzer begins the Anabaptist movement in Germany.

Martin writes: To the Christian Nobility, On the Babylonian Captivity of the Church, and The Freedom of a Christian.

Martin and the students of Wittenberg burn the paper excommunicating him and the books of Roman Catholic Church law.

1521

Martin is declared a heretic at the Diet of Worms.

Martin is kidnapped and held at Wartburg Castle.

Hernando Cortés destroys the Aztec empire and takes over Mexico.

Ferdinand Magellan sails to the Philippines and is killed by the inhabitants.

Pope Leo X dies.

1522

Martin finishes his German translation of the New Testament. 100,000 copies are printed in Wittenberg over the next four decades.

1523

The Reformation's first two martyrs are burned at the stake in Belgium.

1524-1525

German peasants revolt under the leadership of radical Anabaptist leader Thomas Münzer. He is executed at the end of the war.

1525

Martin and Katie marry.

Martin writes Bondage of the Will.

1526

Martin and Katie's first baby, Hans, is born.

Reformation begins in Sweden and Denmark.

1527

Martin writes "A Mighty Fortress is Our God" while his family fights the plague.

Elizabeth Luther is born.

1528

Reformation begins in Scotland.

Martin and Katie bury Elizabeth.

1529

Martin and Ulrich Zwingli argue over Communion at the Marburg Colloquy.

Magdalena Luther is born.

1530

The Protestant Church begins with the Augsburg Confession.

1531

Martin Luther (Jr.) is born.

1532

Reformation begins in France under John Calvin.

1533

Paul Luther is born.

1534

Martin finishes the German translation of the Old Testament.

Margaret Luther is born.

1536

Martin Luther's "Table Talks" is published.

John Calvin's first edition of "Institutes" is published.

Reformation begins in Norway.

William Tyndale is burned at the stake for translating the Bible into English.

1538

Martin writes against the Jews, and again in 1543, angry they do not accept Christ as their Savior.

1541

The Calvinist Reformation begins in Scotland under John Knox.

1542

Magdalena Luther dies. Martin and Katie are distraught.

1545

The Roman Catholic Church condemns the Reformation at the Council of Trent.

1546

Martin Luther dies.

WORKS CONSULTED

Alex, Ben. *Martin Luther: The German Monk Who Changed the Church*. Scandinavia Publishing House: Victor Books/ SP Publications, Inc., 1995.

"Allies or Enemies?" Christian History. Issue 39.

"A Monk Marries." Christian History. Issue 39.

Bainton, Roland H. *Here I Stand: A Life of Martin Luther*. Hendrickson Publishers Marketing, LLC., 1950.

Bainton, Roland H. *The Reformation of the Sixteenth Century*. Beacon Press, 1952, pp. 3-76.

Booth, Edwin P. *Martin Luther: The Great Reformer*. Barbour Publishing, 1995.

Brown, Perry. "Preaching From the Print Shop." Christian History. Issue 34.

Brown, Perry. "Profit-Hungry Printers." Christian History. Issue 34.

Cartwright, Mark. "Medieval Monastery." Ancient History Encyclopedia, https://www.ancient.eu/Medieval_Monastery/. Accessed August 22, 2019.

Cartwright, Mark. "The Daily Life of Medieval Monks." Ancient History Encyclopedia, https://www.ancient.eu/article/1293/the-daily-life-of-medieval-monks/. Accessed August 22, 2019.

Cary, Phillip. "Luther: Gospel, Law, and Reformation." (Lecture Series). The Teaching Company Limited Partnership, 2004.

"Catholic Encyclopedia: Martin Luther". http://www.newadvent.org/cathen/09438b.htm, Accessed March 1, 2012.

Chalmers, Alexander and Luther, Martin, Haslitt, Esq, William, ed., *The Table Talk of Martin Luther*, (London: Bell & Daldy, 1872), pp. 152-153.

"Christianity for Common Folk." Christian History. Issue 39.

"The Decisive Documents of 1520." Christian History. Issue 34.

Dillenberger, John, Ed. *Martin Luther: Selections from his Writings*. Doubleday, 1961.

Doak, Robin S. Pope *Leo X: Opponent of the Reformation*. Compass Point Books, 2006.

"From the Editor: The Forgotten Years of Martin Luther." Christian History. Issue 39.

Dowley, Tim. Atlas of the European Reformations. Fortress Press, 2015.

Duffy, Eamon. Saints and Sinners: A History of the Popes. Yale University Press, 2006, pp. 177-208.

Durant, Will. The Reformation. Simon & Schuster, 1957, pp. 293-402.

"Empires". Martin Luther. [DVD] Prod. PBS Home Video, 2002.

Fearon, Mike. Martin Luther. Bethany House Publishers, 1986.

Flowers, Sarah. The Reformation. Lucent Books, 1996.

Galli, Mark. "Martin Luther's Later Years: Did You Know?." Christian History. Issue 39.

Galli, Mark. "The Weak Man Behind a Mighty Fortress." Christian History. Issue 39.

George, Timothy Dr. "Dr. Luther's Theology." Christian History. Issue 34.

Grant, George and Wilbur, Gregory. The Christian Almanac. Cumberland House, 2004.

Gregory, Brad S. "The History of Christianity in the Reformation Era, Part 1." (Lecture) The Teaching Company Limited Partnership, 2001.

Grime, Paul J. "Changing the Tempo of Worship." Christian History. Issue 39.

Grun, Bernard. The Timetables of History. Simon & Schuster, 1963.

Gyldenvand, Lily M. Martin Luther: Giant of Faith. Augsburg Publishing House, 1981.

Hendrix, Dr. Scott A. "Legends About Luther." Christian History. Issue 34.

His Career. Augsburg Publishing House, 1986.

Kittleson, James M. Dr. "What Was Luther's World Like?" Christian History. Issue 34.

Klug, Dr. Eugemne F.A. "Luther's Will and Testaments." Christian History. Issue 39.

MacCuish, D

History. Issue 39.

Miller, Kevin A. "From the Editor: Dwarfed by a Giant." Christian History. Issue 34.

Norwich, John Julius. Absolute Monarchs: A History of the Papacy. Random House, 2011, pp. 275-298.

Oberman, Dr. Heiko A. "Fool in Rome." Christian History. Issue 34.

O'Malley, John W., SJ. A History of the Popes: From Peter to the Present. Rowman & Littlefield Publishers, Inc., 2010, pp. 171-187.

"Peasant's War". http://en.wikipedia.org/wiki/Peasants'_War, Accessed February 1, 2010.

"Powerful Preaching." Christian History. Issue 39.

"Protestants' Most-Famous Document." Christian History. Issue 34.

"Reinventing Family Life." Christian History. Issue 39.

Robbert, Dr. George S. "Martin Luther's Early Years: Recommended Resources." Christian History. Issue 34.

Robbert, Dr. George S. "Martin Luther's Later Years: Recommended Resources." Christian History. Issue 39.

Rowling, Marjorie. Life in Medieval Times. Capricorn Books, 1973, pp. 113-134.

Sanders, Ruth H. German: Biography of a Language. Oxford University Press, 2010, pp. 117-156.

Schurb, Ken. "Martin Luther's Early Years: Christian History Timeline." Christian History. Issue 34.

Schurb, Ken. "Martin Luther's Later Years: Christian History Timeline." Christian History. Issue 39.

Schwiebert, E.G. Luther and His Times: The Reformation from a New Perspective. Concordia Publishing House, 1950.

Spitz, Dr. Lewis W. "The Political Luther." Christian History. Issue 34.

"The 95 Theses by Martin Luther". http://www.reformed.org/documents/index.html?mainframe=http://www.reformed.org/documents/95_theses.html, Accessed February 16, 2010.

Thigpen, Paul. "Luther's Political Allies." Christian History. Issue 34.

Thigpen, Paul. "Luther's Political Nemesis." Christian History. Issue 34.

Thigpen, Paul. "Martin Luther's Early Years: A Gallery of Friends and Enemies." Christian History. Issue 34.

Thigpen, Paul. "The Parents Luther Feared Disgracing." Christian History. Issue 34.

Tucker, Ruth A. Parade of the Faith: A Biographical History of the Christian Church. Zondervan, 2011, pp. 217-238.

"The Unrefined Reformer." Christian History. Issue 39.

"Was Luther Anti-Semitic?." Christian History. Issue 39.

Zecher, Henry. "The Bible Translation That Rocked the World." Christian History. Issue 34.

Other books in the series

What was the Gutenberg Bible?

Why did the Reformation Happen?

CHRISTIAN FOCUS PUBLICATIONS

Christian Focus | Christian Heritage | CF4K | Mentor

CF4·K
Because you're never
too young to know Jesus

Christian Focus Publications publishes books for adults and children under its four main imprints: Christian Focus, CF4K, Mentor and Christian Heritage. Our books reflect our conviction that God's Word is reliable and Jesus is the way to know him, and live for ever with him.

Our children's publication list covers pre-school to early teens. We also publish personal and family devotional titles, biographies and inspirational stories that children will love.

From pre-school board books to teenage apologetics, we have it covered!

Christian Focus Publications Ltd,
Geanies House, Fearn, Ross-shire,
IV20 1TW, Scotland,
United Kingdom.
www.christianfocus.com